Vicki Lansky's

KIDS COOKING

SCHOLASTIC INC.
New York Toronto London Auckland Sydney

other titles by Vicki Lansky include:

FEED ME I'M YOURS
TAMING OF THE CANDY MONSTER
DEAR BABYSITTER HANDBOOK
PRACTICAL PARENTING books
KOKO BEAR Read-Together books

Special thanks for recipe testing goes to:
Dana W. Lansky
Kathy Jopling and her
students at Breck School, Minneapolis, MN

Photography: Harlan Graphics
Food stylist: Suzanne Lang
Art direction & design: MacLean and Tuminelly
Editor: Eva Moore
Editorial assistant: Susan Krajac

ISBN 0-590-40624-8

12 11 10 9 8 7 6 5 4 3

Printed in the U.S.A.

7 8 9/8 0 1 2/9

23

First Scholastic printing, September 1987

TABLE OF CONTENTS

DESSERTS

Ice Cream and Cookie Pie
(page 6)

Over-The-Rainbow Cloud
(page 14)

Brownie Fudge Favorites
(page 12)

Lemony Cheese Cake Bars
(page 10)

Tart-Riffic Delights
(page 8)

SNACKS

Peanut Butter Roll-Ups
(page 22)

Banana Smoothie
(page 24)

Handy Oatmeal Cookies
(page 20)

Ants On A Log
(page 18)

Bird Nest Clusters
(page 16)

MINI-MEALS

Tutti-Fruitti Fruit Salad
(page 30)

Mexican Mix Casserole
(page 32)

Oven French Toast
(page 28)

Stone Soup
(page 26)

Tuna Sail Boats
(page 34)

HOLIDAY TREATS

Valentine Jell-O® Jiggle Hearts
(page 36)

Easter Bunny Bread
(page 38)

Holiday Snack Tree
(page 42)

Halloween Jack-O-Lantern Frosties
(page 40)

BEFORE YOU START

B • • • Be sure to check with an adult about the use of the kitchen and especially the use of an oven.

E • • • Equipment should all be out and ready before you begin cooking.

F • • • First, wash your hands before handling food.

O • • • Opt for an apron to keep your clothes clean and give you something to wipe your hands on.

R • • • Read through ingredient lists and instructions at least once before you start any recipe.

E • • • Easier to ask adults for help or advice before you begin than while you're in the middle of a recipe.

Please read the tip (like this one) at the end of each recipe before you begin. It may give you an idea that you would like to use.

AFTER YOU'RE DONE

A...Always clean up after yourself immediately. If you wait, food hardens, and dishes, utensils and countertops become harder to clean. A good cook always cleans up little by little while cooking.

F...Foil or plastic wrap should be used to cover all foods and finished recipes.

T...Turn off the oven.

E...Everything needs to be returned to its original place.

R...Remember that clean counter tops and tables are part of the clean-up process.

THINK SAFETY

S...Serrated knives are safer to use than dull knives or fine slicing knives. Cut away from you and use a cutting board.

A...Always wipe up floor spills immediately to prevent slips and falls.

F...Fires that start from grease-cooking can be extinquished by covering with baking soda -- NOT WATER!

E...Easy-to-reach pot holders or oven gloves are a must.

T...Turn handles of saucepans and pots toward the center of the stove so you won't bump them.

Y...You should never cook with heat (oven, stove top, or microwave) without the knowledge and permission of an adult.

ANYTHING THAT CAN BE TURNED ON — MUST BE TURNED OFF!

HOW TO MEASURE

Wet things: Fill the measuring spoon or cup to the top. Use a glass measuring cup like this:

| one cup | ½ cup | ⅓ cup | ¼ cup |

Dry things: Fill the measuring spoon or individual cup over the top then scrape the extra food off the top and make it level. Use individual cups like:

| one cup | ½ cup | ⅓ cup | ¼ cup |

one Tablespoon (Tbsp)   one teaspoon (tsp)   ½ tsp   ¼ tsp

DID YOU KNOW THAT "this" EQUALS "that":

this	= that
3 teaspoons	= 1 Tablespoon
4 Tablespoons	= ¼ cup
5 Tablespoons + 1 teaspoon	= ⅓ cup
16 Tablespoons	= 1 cup
1 cup	= 8 ounces
2 cups	= 1 pint
4 cups	= 1 quart
2 quarts	= ½ gallon
1 stick margarine	= ½ cup or ¼ pound or 8 Tablespoons
60 minutes	= 1 hour

DESSERTS

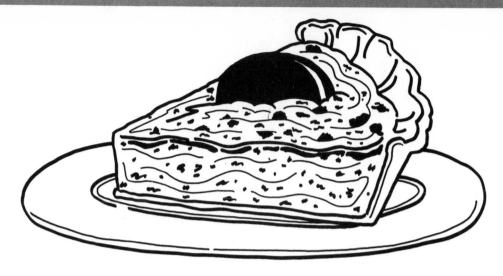

Ice Cream and Cookie Pie

HERE'S WHAT YOU NEED
(Take out all items before beginning)

1 ready-made pie crust of graham crackers or chocolate crumbs

1-quart container of vanilla ice cream (or 2 one-pint containers)

4 granola bars or oatmeal cookies or another favorite such as Oreos®

plastic bag and twist-tie

large mixing bowl

heavy-duty spoon

freezer wrap

rolling pin

HERE'S WHAT YOU DO

(First, read steps 1-8)

 **1.** Remove container of ice cream from the freezer and let it soften for 15 minutes to a ½ hour.

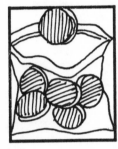 **2.** Take cookies and place them in a large, strong plastic bag. Close bag and lay it on a flat surface.

 **3.** Using a rolling pin or the base of a small bowl or sturdy glass, roll or pound the cookies in the bag until they are crushed.

 **4.** Put softened ice cream into a large mixing bowl and add the cookie crumbs from the plastic bag into the bowl.

 **5.** Using the heavy-duty spoon, slowly mix the crumbs into the softened ice cream.

 **6.** Pour or spoon this mixture into ready-made pie crust. Spread gently from the center to the sides.

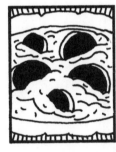 **7.** Top with additional crumbs or candies, if you wish.

 **8.** Cover the ice cream pie with foil freeze wrap or with the cover from the ready-made crust reversed and put the pie in the freezer for at least 2 hours before serving.

Cookies or candies or chips can also be chopped into bits and pieces using a blender. This recipe is a wonderful way to use up any last-in-the-box, ready-to-be crumbled cookies!

Tart-Riffic Delights

HERE'S WHAT YOU NEED
(Take out all items before beginning)

1 package (3½ ounces) instant vanilla pudding and pie filling

2 cups cold milk

1 package (6 shells) single serving crust shells (4 ounces)

1½ to 2 cups any combination of favorite fresh fruits such as: blueberries, strawberries (sliced), red or green seedless grapes, cut-up kiwi or sliced peaches

¼ cup apple jelly

1 medium size mixing bowl

1 medium size plate

small saucepan

spoon

pastry brush

HERE'S WHAT YOU DO

(First, read steps 1-8)

 **1.** Combine instant pudding and cold milk in a mixing bowl, according to package directions.

 **2.** On a plate, set out approximately two cups of any fresh fruits you wish to use. Pick fruits with different colors to make the tarts more attractive.

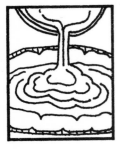 **3.** Using a spoon, fill each tart halfway full with the pudding.

 **4.** Arrange fruit on top of the pudding in an attractive pattern. (Use a spoon or your clean hands.)

 **5.** Measure out a ¼ cup of apple jelly and put it into a small saucepan.

 **6.** Place the saucepan on the stove and melt the apple jelly over low heat for 15 minutes or until melted. Stir occasionally.

 **7.** Using a pastry brush, spread the apple jelly over the fruit tarts for a pretty glaze. (Carefully pour extra apple jelly back into the jar. It will reset.)

 **8.** Chill for at least one hour before serving.

Canned, sliced fruits that have been drained and rinsed with water also work just fine if fresh fruits aren't available.

Lemony Cheese Cake Bars

HERE'S WHAT YOU NEED

(Take out all items before beginning)

1 package refrigerated crescent dinner rolls

2 packages (8 ounces each) of cream cheese

3 Tablespoons lemon juice (fresh or concentrated)

1 teaspoon vanilla flavoring

¾ cup of sugar

3 eggs

medium- to large-size mixing bowl

mixing spoon or electric mixer

measuring cup

Tablespoon

teaspoon

8 x12 inch shallow baking dish

knife

10

HERE'S WHAT YOU DO

(First, read steps 1-8)

 **1.** Preheat oven to 350 degrees F.

 **2.** Put the cream cheese in the mixing bowl and let it soften for ½ hour. Or, soften in the micro-wave for 1 minute.

 **3.** Add 3 Table-spoons lemon juice, 1 teaspoon vanilla flavoring, ¾ cup sugar and 3 eggs to the softened cream cheese.

 **4.** Mix well with a large spoon or elec-tic mixer until blended. (Small lumps are okay.)

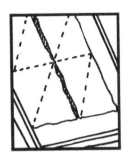 **5.** Open package of rolls according to directions. Unroll dough and spread out pieces in the baking dish so they touch and form a large rectangle.

 **6.** With your fin-gers, press dough edges together until the bottom of the baking dish is cov-ered.

 **7.** Pour the cream cheese mixture over the dough to edges.

 **8.** Bake in the oven for 30 minutes. Re-move, let cool, then refrigerate before cut-ting into bars. Store covered in the refrig-erator.

Make ordinary bars less ordinary by cutting them at an angle and creating diamond-shaped or triangle-shaped pieces as pictured on page 10.

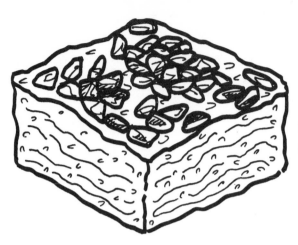

Fudge Brownie Favorites

HERE'S WHAT YOU NEED

(Take out all items before beginning)

1 package (8 ounces)
   semi-sweet chocolate pieces

1 can (14 ounces) sweetened
   condensed milk

1 teaspoon vanilla

1 cup pieces of nuts
   (preferrably walnuts)

2 cups honey crunch (toasted)
   wheat germ

microwave oven

8 inch square glass pan

1 cup measuring cup

large mixing spoon

knife

HERE'S WHAT YOU DO

(First, read steps 1-8)

 **1.** Place semi-sweet chocolate pieces in a glass or microwave-proof bowl.

 **5.** Stir gently until well blended within the pan.

 **2.** Melt on high for 2 minutes or until very soft. Remove from oven.

 **6.** Using a knife or spoon, press mixture down and evenly around the pan.

 **3.** Add the condensed milk and vanilla to the melted chocolate and stir until well mixed.

 **7.** Press all the remaining nuts into the top of the mixture.

 **4.** Add wheat germ and half the nuts to the mixture.

 **8.** Let stand at room temperature until firm. Or, if you're in a hurry, put it into the refrigerator for an hour.

No microwave? No problem! In an oven melt the chocolate pieces in a pan to be used for this recipe for 15 minutes at 350 degrees F. or until the chocolate is very soft.

Over-The-Rainbow Cloud

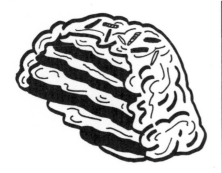

HERE'S WHAT YOU NEED

(Take out all items before beginning)

1 box of chocolate wafer cookies

1 can (7 or 14 ounces) pressurized whipped cream

1 container of colored sprinkles

spreading knife

narrow dish

HERE'S WHAT YOU DO

(First, read steps 1-3)

1. Spray whipped cream on one side of a cookie and set it on a plate. Spray another cookie and stick it on the first. Keep doing this until you have a stack of five. Then turn the the stack on edge to make the start of a "log." Continue adding as many cookies as you have room for.

2. Refrigerate at least 4 hours before serving so cookies will soften.

3. When ready to serve, spread with more whipped cream to cover cookie log completely. Add colored sprinkles. Cut diagonally so each piece is striped.

14

SNACKS

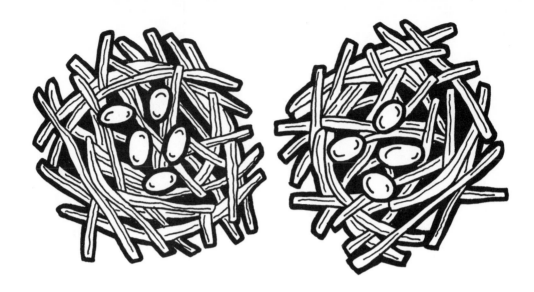

Bird Nest Clusters

HERE'S WHAT YOU NEED

(Take out all items before beginning)

1 package (12 ounces or 1½ cups) semi-sweet chocolate chips

½ cup peanut butter ("chunky" is better if you have a choice)

4 cups chow mein noodles (or a 6 ounce bag)

Colored candies (optional)

large glass bowl

waxed paper

mixing spoon or fork

2 cookie trays

16

HERE'S WHAT YOU DO

(First, read steps 1-6)

 **1.** Put the chocolate chips and peanut butter into a large glass or microwave-proof bowl. Set the timer for 1 minute. Or melt them in the oven in a cooking pan at 350 degrees F.

 **2.** Remove the mixture and stir. Place it back in the oven for 1½ minutes, or until chocolate chips are completely melted.

 **3.** Add the chow mein noodles.

 **4.** Mix the noodles by using one or two forks or spoons as though you were tossing a salad to get them evenly coated with the chocolate/peanut butter mixture.

 **5.** Lay a piece of waxed paper over two cookie sheets.

 **6.** Drop golf-ball size clusters on the covered cookie sheet to cool and set. Add a few colored candies as "eggs" to the nests!

If you chill these in the refrigerator, it speeds up the hardening time so you can eat them sooner.

Ants On A Log

HERE'S WHAT YOU NEED

(Take out all items before beginning)

Bunch of celery   *paper towel*

1 container of peanut butter   *knife*

½ cup of raisins   *plate*

HERE'S WHAT YOU DO

(First, read steps 1-7)

 **1.** Pull the celery stalks apart.

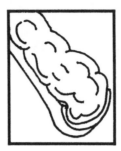 **5.** Fill each celery "log" with peanut butter and spread it over the length of the "log" so it fills it all up.

 **2.** Cut off leafy top of stalks and cut off the bottom section.

 **6.** Place 5-10 raisins on top of the peanut butter in each celery stalk. (These are the ants.)

 **3.** Wash each piece under cold water and dry on a paper towel.

 **7.** Cut each "log" into 2 or 3 sections and place them on a plate.

 **4.** Using the knife, scoop out a knifeful of the peanut butter.

You could put chocolate chips on the "logs" instead of the raisins, although it would not be as nutritious . . . but we won't tell!

19

Handy Oatmeal Cookies

HERE'S WHAT YOU NEED

(Take out all items before beginning)

3 sticks of butter or margarine
   (1½ cups)

3 cups of old-fashioned oatmeal

1½ cups brown sugar

1½ cups flour

1½ teaspoons baking powder

large mixing bowl

measuring cup

cookie sheet

clean hands (yours!)

*knife or spatula for taking
   cookies off cookie sheet*

HERE'S WHAT YOU DO

(First, read steps 1-8)

 **1.** Turn on oven to 350 degrees F.

 **2.** Place butter or margarine in the bottom of the large mixing bowl. Let stand at room temperature for ½ hour to soften or put it in your microwave oven (on low) for one minute.

 **3.** Add the oatmeal, brown sugar, flour and baking powder to the softened butter or margarine.

4. Using your hands, mix it . . . mash it . . . squish it . . . pound it . . . until all the ingredients are mixed together. Now mix it some more.

 **5.** Next, take a small piece of the cookie dough and roll it into a small ball about the size of a ping-pong ball.

 **6.** Place the ball on a cookie sheet and continue to make more balls, placing them 2 inches apart.

 **7.** Bake for 10 minutes.

 **8.** Using pot holders, remove cookie sheet and finished cookies from the oven. Let them cool for 15 minutes on the cookie sheet before taking them off and putting them on a plate or they will crumble.

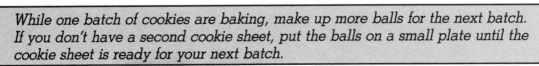

While one batch of cookies are baking, make up more balls for the next batch. If you don't have a second cookie sheet, put the balls on a small plate until the cookie sheet is ready for your next batch.

21

Peanut Butter Roll-Ups

HERE'S WHAT YOU NEED

(Take out all items before beginning)

1 container of peanut butter	*knife*
4 slices of bread	*rolling pin*
Honey or jam	*toothpicks*

HERE'S WHAT YOU DO

(First, read steps 1-7)

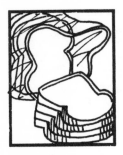 **1.** Remove 4 slices of bread from a package of sliced bread.

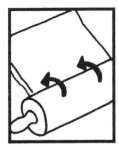 **2.** Using the knife, cut off crusts from each piece of bread. (You can feed them to the birds.)

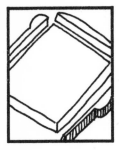 **3.** Place each piece on a hard surface and roll them flat with the rolling pin.

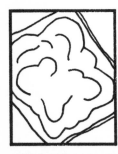 **4.** Spread a thin layer of peanut butter on the flattened pieces of bread with a knife.

 **5.** Spread on some jam or maybe drizzle some honey on top of the peanut butter.

 **6.** Roll each piece of bread from the bottom up, jelly-roll style.

 **7.** Slice roll into one-inch pieces and insert tooth picks to hold the roll-ups in place.

There are really many variations you can try with this food-fix-in' technique. You can use cream cheese instead of peanut butter; cinnamon instead of jam or honey. Use your imagination!

Banana Smoothie

HERE'S WHAT YOU NEED

(Take out all items before beginning)

1 banana
1 cup of milk
½ teaspoon of vanilla
Ice cubes (1-3 of them)

blender
glass measuring cup

HERE'S WHAT YOU DO

(First, read steps 1-4)

 **1.** Take out the blender and pour in one cup of milk.

 **3.** Add ½ teaspoon vanilla and ice cubes.

 **2.** Peel the banana, break it in half and add to milk in blender.

 **4.** Blend for 20 seconds; pour into a glass — serve and enjoy!

The riper the banana — or the more brown spots it has on the peel — the sweeter it is and the better it is for you. Just because a banana has spots on the peel doesn't mean it has spots on the inside.

MINI-MEALS

26
Stone Soup

28
Oven French Toast

30
Tutti-Frutti Fruit Salad

32
Mexican Mix Casserole

34
Tuna Sail Boats

Stone Soup

HERE'S WHAT YOU NEED

(Take out all items before beginning)

1 medium-sized potato

1 carrot

1 stalk celery

1 slice of onion to make
   2 Tablespoons of chopped
   onions

1 can (10¾ ounces) condensed
   chicken broth

1 can of water

can opener

*2-quart pot with a handle
   and a cover*

stove

knife

measuring cup

peeler

ladle or large spoon

soup bowls

HERE'S WHAT YOU DO

(First, read steps 1-8)

 **1.** Open can of chicken broth and pour contents into pot. Fill the can with water and add it to the pot.

 **2.** Peel potato with a knife or peeler. Place potato (your "stone") in the pot. (It should be covered — or almost covered — by the liquid. If not, your pot is too shallow and you need a different pot.)

3. Place pot on stove over a high heat.

 **4.** Peel and cut carrot and celery into one-inch sections. Add to the pot.

 **5.** Chop onion to make approximately 2 Tablespoons and add to the pot.

 **6.** When the soup comes to a boil, reduce the heat to medium, cover and let it cook on the stove top for 30 minutes. (Set your timer.)

 **7.** Test potato with a fork. If it seems soft, the soup is done.

 **8.** Turn off heat when done and ladle the soup into bowls and serve. (You can eat the "stone" yourself or divide it and share it.)

You can add soup toppings when you are done, such as chopped chives, bacon bits or croutons, if you like.

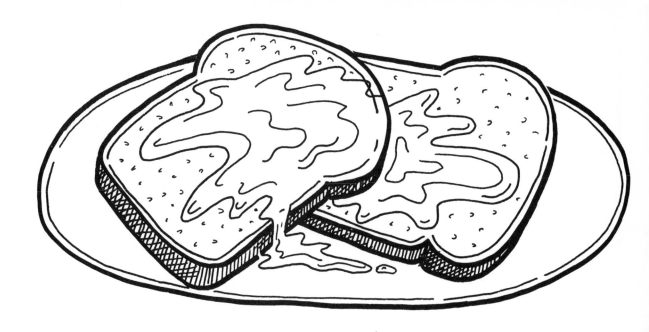

Oven French Toast

HERE'S WHAT YOU NEED

(Take out all items before beginning)

4 eggs

½ cup milk

½ teaspoon vanilla flavoring

8 slices of bread: whole wheat
or white

Pat of butter or margarine

fork

bowl or dish with a wide base

measuring cup

cookie sheet

spatula

pot holders or oven mitts

HERE'S WHAT YOU DO

(First, read steps 1-8)

 **1.** Turn oven on to 300 degrees F. Lightly grease the cookie sheet with butter or margarine.

 **2.** Crack eggs into a shallow bowl. (Make sure to pick out any bits of shell.)

 **3.** Add milk and vanilla flavoring to eggs and mix all together with a fork.

4. Using a fork, dip both sides of bread into the mixture, and place on the cookie sheet. Pour any remaining egg mixture over the bread.

 **5.** Place in the oven to bake for 10 minutes.(Set your timer.)

 **6.** After 10 minutes, remove cookie sheet using pot holders. Using a spatula, turn each piece of bread over.

 **7.** Return cookie sheet with bread slices to the oven for another 5 minutes.

8. With the pot holders, remove from the oven and using the spatula, place pieces of Oven French Toast on a serving dish. Serve with any of the following: maple syrup, cinnamon, jam, or brown sugar.

Wrap any left-over pieces in clear plastic wrap and place in the freezer. When ready to use, simply unwrap, re-heat in toaster or microwave.

Tutti-Fruitti Fruit Salad

HERE'S WHAT YOU NEED

(Take out all items before beginning)

3 cans of fruit (11-16 ounces):
    mandarin orange sections
    pineapple chunks
    sliced pears

1 medium banana

1 cup mini-marshmallows

1 cup (8 ounce container) of
    sour cream

large bowl

large mixing spoon

strainer

knife

can opener

measuring cup

HERE'S WHAT YOU DO

(First, read steps 1-8)

 **1.** Place the cup of sour cream into the large bowl.

 **5.** Add all the drained, canned fruit pieces into the bowl.

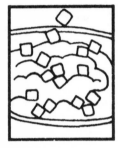 **2.** Add the mini-marshmallows.

 **6.** Peel banana and slice into ½-inch circles. Add to bowl.

 **3.** Open cans of fruit with the can opener.

 **7.** Mix all ingredients gently with a large spoon until the sour cream seems to cover everything.

 **4.** Partially block off the top of the can with the lid and pour out liquid into the sink.

 **8.** Cover the bowl and chill in refrigerator before serving. (If you are really hungry, you can eat it without chilling it!)

You can vary this recipe by substituting any fruits you have in the house or with ones you like better. You can use fresh fruits, too. If you like shredded coconut, 1 cup makes a nice addition to the salad.

Mexican Mix Casserole

HERE'S WHAT YOU NEED

(Take out all items before beginning)

1 can (15 ounces) of chili

1 can (12 or 17 ounces) of
   whole kernel corn

1 package (8 ounces) of grated
   cheese or grate one cup of
   brick cheddar cheese

1 to 2 cups crumbed corn or
   nacho chips (or 7½ ounce
   bag)

can opener

*medium size baking dish (glass
   if cooking in microwave)*

strainer

spoon or knife

cheese grater

pot holders

HERE'S WHAT YOU DO

(First, read steps 1-8)

 **1.** Heat oven to 350 degrees F.

 **5.** Add grated cheese to the casserole. There is no need to mix up the casserole.

 **2.** Open can of chili and empty into the casserole dish.

 **6.** Crumble chips in your hands over the top of the casserole and press them down gently, part way into the mixture.

 **3.** Open the can of corn and pour out liquid by partially blocking the top of the can with the lid.

 **7.** Bake in the oven for 20 minutes. Remove from oven using pot holders.

 **4.** Add the corn to the chili.

 **8.** Serve casserole with extra whole chips, if you wish.

Make the casserole in a square or round glass dish, and you can cook it in a microwave oven for 4 minutes on high for an even faster meal.

HERE'S WHAT YOU NEED

(Take out all items before beginning)

1 can (6½ ounces) of tuna fish	*can opener*
2 small green peppers	*medium mixing bowl*
½ cup mayonnaise	*fork knife*
Single cheese slices for sails	*toothpicks*

HERE'S WHAT YOU DO

(First, read steps 1-4)

1. Open can of tuna fish. Over the sink, squeeze lid into meat, forcing the liquid out to drain tuna. Pour tuna into bowl and mix with ½ cup mayonnaise.

3. Fill both halves with the tuna mixture.

2. Cut green pepper in half lengthwise and remove insides using your fingers and also rinsing with water.

4. Slice cheese squares diagonally and weave a toothpick through each piece. Insert in the "boats" as the sails.

Green peppers not your favorite food? You can also make Tuna Boats in scooped-out baked potatoes, pita bread or even hot dog buns!

HOLIDAY TREATS

36
Valentine Jell-O®
Jiggle Hearts

38
Easter Bunny Bread

40
Halloween Jack-O-Lantern
Frosties

42
Holiday Snack Tree

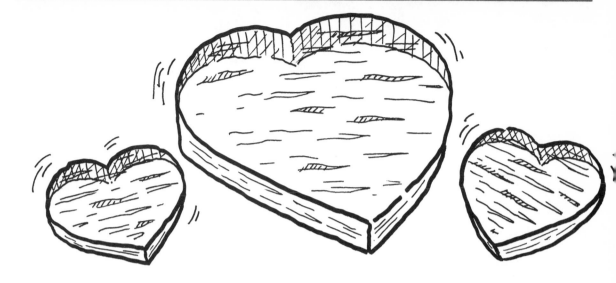

Valentine Jell-O®
Jiggle Hearts

HERE'S WHAT YOU NEED

(Take out all items before beginning)

2 envelopes unflavored gelatin

2½ cups water

1 package (6 ounces) Jell-O® (cherry, strawberry or raspberry)

Pat of butter or margarine

medium size mixing bowl

measuring cup

medium size saucepan

spoon

small shallow pan such as an 8 inch square

one heart-shaped cookie cutter

HERE'S WHAT YOU DO

(First, read steps 1-8)

 **1.** Fill a small bowl with one cup of cool water.

 **2.** Cut the corners off the 2 envelopes of unflavored gelatin and pour the powdered gelatin into the water. Stir until partially dissolved and set aside.

 **3.** In a medium saucepan, bring one cup of water to a boil and add Jell-O® powder from box. Be careful with the hot water!

 **4.** Bring the mixture to a boil again for just a second (or it will boil over) and remove from heat immediately.

 **5.** Carefully add hot Jell-O® to the bowl and then stir together until dissolved. (Place hot saucepan in sink and fill with hot water to make cleanup easier.)

 **6.** Add ½ cup cold water to the mixture.

7. Very lightly grease the pan with a bit of butter or margarine and pour mixture into the pan. Refrigerate until firm. (Takes at least four hours.)

8. Cut the Jell-O® with heart-shaped cookie cutters. Store covered in the refrigerator. (The cook gets to eat the in-between Jell-O® pieces left!)

You can speed up the jelling process by adding six ice cubes for step #6 instead of the cold water. Stir the mixture till the ice cubes are dissolved.

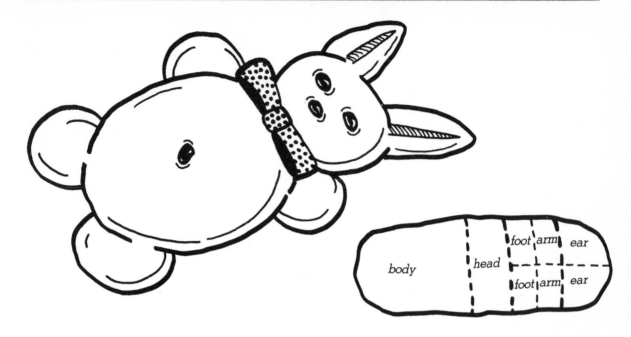

body · head · foot · arm · ear · foot · arm · ear

Easter Bunny Bread

HERE'S WHAT YOU NEED

(Take out all items before beginning)

1 loaf of frozen bread dough
   (16 ounces)

1 egg

4 raisins

Pat of margarine or butter

clean hands

cookie sheet

knife

small bowl for egg

fork

pastry brush

ribbon

HERE'S WHAT YOU DO

(First, read steps 1-10)

1. Thaw frozen bread dough at room temperature for 3 hours or defrost overnight in the refrigerator.

2. Grease a large cookie sheet using butter or margarine.

3. Cut the thawed dough into 2 equal pieces. Shape first piece into large flat oval for Bunny's body.

4. Cut the remaining half into 3 sections. Shape one section into a round ball for Bunny's head. Cut one section in half and shape into oval Bunny ears.

5. Cut the last section into four equal pieces and shape 2 pieces into ovals for feet and 2 into balls for front paws. Attach to the body.

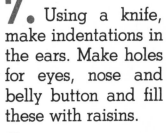

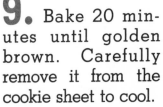

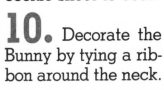

6. Let the Bunny dough rise in an undrafty place for one hour or two, until the dough is almost double in size. After dough has risen, preheat oven to 375 degrees F.

7. Using a knife, make indentations in the ears. Make holes for eyes, nose and belly button and fill these with raisins.

8. Crack egg into small bowl. Beat it lightly with a fork and brush the Bunny with the beaten egg using the pastry brush.

9. Bake 20 minutes until golden brown. Carefully remove it from the cookie sheet to cool.

10. Decorate the Bunny by tying a ribbon around the neck.

Halloween Jack-O-Lantern Frosties

HERE'S WHAT YOU NEED

(Take out all items before beginning)

4-6 navel oranges

1 (8 ounces) container of
vanilla or plain yogurt

Icing tubes or cans of several
colors

Mini-marshmallows, silver
decors, colored candies,
gum drops, green-colored
cherries or pineapple

serrated knife

grapefruit spoon

blender

straws

HERE'S WHAT YOU DO

(First, read steps 1-8)

 **1.** Cut a thin slice of peel from the bottom of each orange so it will not roll.

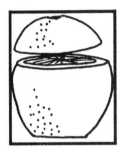 **2.** Slice off the top 1/3 of each orange.

 **3.** Scoop out the inside with the knife and a grapefruit spoon.

 **4.** Put the pulp and juice (minus seeds) into the blender.

 **5.** Add container of yogurt to blender and mix well.

 **6.** Wipe orange dry, decorate each orange shell like a Jack-O-Lantern using tubed frosting and decors. A green gum drop or colored cherry or pineapple makes a good "stem."

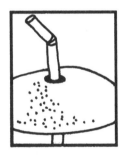 **7.** Cut a small hole in each "cap" and insert a straw which has been cut in half.

 **8.** Pour drink from blender into Jack-O-Lantern cups and serve.

You can cut off the "cap" in a zig-zag pattern to look more like a Jack-O-Lantern. It might help to outline this pattern first with a marker.

Holiday Snack Tree

HERE'S WHAT YOU NEED

(Take out all items before beginning)

1 package of favorite hard
   cheese (Swiss, cheddar, etc.)

1 basket of cherry tomatoes

1 bunch of grapes

1 small head of cauliflower

1 green pepper

2 carrots

dip ingredients: 1-pint container
   (16 ounces) of sour cream 1
   envelope of Lipton® onion
   soup mix

*styrofoam cone about 12 inches
   high*

*green metallic or holiday
   wrapping paper*

cutting board

sharp knife

toothpicks

small mixing bowl

plate

HERE'S WHAT YOU DO

(First, read steps 1-8)

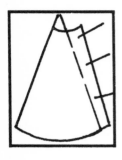 **1.** Make the base for the Holiday Snack Tree by covering styrofoam cone with holiday foil or wrapping paper. Hold paper in place using toothpicks or tape.

 **2.** Cut cheese into 1-inch cubes on a cutting board.

 **3.** Wash and pull apart the head of cauliflower.

 **4.** Wash grapes, green pepper and carrots and cut the last two into bite-sized chunks.

 **5.** Push toothpicks halfway into one or more food pieces in any order you please.

 **6.** Stick the toothpicks attached with edibles into the styrofoam tree.

 **7.** In a small bowl, blend the dry soup mix with sour cream and chill.

 **8.** Place the snack tree on a plate; set out with dip, and invite everyone to serve themselves.

Any other favorite family dip — or even a store-bought one — can also work just fine here.

RECIPE NOTES

Make up your own recipes or copy recipes you want to keep.

RECIPE NOTES

Make up your own recipes or copy recipes you want to keep.

RECIPE NOTES

Make up your own recipes or copy recipes you want to keep.